Mistress/female slave BDSM Contract

Warning - *Even if a Spanking and/or BDSM contract is not considered legally binding in your country/locality, attempts may be made to include parts of it in law enforcement or other legal proceedings, should their involvement ever occur for some reason. "Consent" could be a defense to assault in many places (though not necessarily effective.) A legal argument might be attempted stating that by signing the contract you are agreeing to everything in it. Also, in areas of the world where some or all BDSM activities are illegal, contracts of any sort can be used to prosecute those involved.*

By Mistress

Copyright © 2013

ISBN-13: 978-1482578355
ISBN-10: 1482578352

Erotic BDSM Books - Your Erotic BDSM Book Publisher
EroticBDSMbooks.com

Included in this publication is the book "*The Spanking Dictionary*".

Other BDSM Books by Phil G. Include:

Table of Contents

Bonus – "The Spanking Dictionary" (adult erotica)

Introduction

This collection is only a guide. You should add, subtract and adapt rules as desired. There is ample room for that. If you live with others, such as children, it's likely many rules will at least need to be adapted.

By going through this contract you'll learn a lot about what BDSM experiences each person is into, or might be interested in getting into. Remember you can change the contract at anytime. There is extra space at the end of each section for you to write your own entries, if that is your wish.

Make sure to cross out and replace wording you don't want, then you both initial that entry.

This contract and its collection of rules are based on the Dominant being female and the submissive/slave being female.

The term "*slave*" in this book is used interchangeably with the terms "*sub*" and "*submissive*".

The term "*Dominant*" is used interchangeably with "*Mistress*".

Dominants may wish to test their submissive\slave on how well she remembers the rules and knows the specifics of the contract. (Good news, you now have a wonderful excuse to spank your slave if she forgets something from the contract!)

These rules are not presented in order of their importance.

Trust, care, mutual consent, safe sex practices, and general safety are absolute priorities. No matter what it's suggested that you incorporate at least the following into your playtime and lifestyle:

- Don't tie things around someone's neck, and no breath play, period!
- Create a "Safe word" for the submissive to say when (or if) things get too scary.
- Always be careful and take necessary safety precautions when engaging in BDSM activity. Keep proper medical facilities handy.
- Always insure that a bound person has adequate circulation. If the person tied up has to go to the bathroom or has physical problems, that person must be immediately released from bondage.
- Ask about medical issues before playing and adjust your playing activities according to any medical issues.
- Never leave anyone bound and alone.
- Understand what a gagged person sounds like in sexual ecstasy versus in pain.
- Do not play while under the influence of drugs or alcohol.
- Always check that your handcuffs and/or lock keys work before playing. If you have to go to the locksmith to get the handcuffs off, it's going to be embarrassing.
- When removing someone from bondage, allow them to move their own limbs.
- If pregnant or ill, check with your doctor before engaging in BDSM related activity.
- Always play within your own skill base and comfort level.

Mistress/slave BDSM Contract
(Feel free to change and adapt those areas of the contract as you see fit.)

I, _____ (slave), hereinafter referred to as "girl",

agree to submit to:

_____ , hereinafter referred to as "Mistress".

The girl understands that her submission is voluntary and includes sexual submission, BDSM play including bondage and discipline subject to the terms and conditions set forth in this contract.

The girl and her Mistress agree to the terms as stated in this contract.

Having read and understood this contract, the Mistress and slave sign this contract freely and without reservation.

The term (length) of this contract is for _____ days from the date of signing.

_____

MISTRESS   DATE

_____

SLAVE   DATE

_____

Witness (optional)   DATE

_____

Witness (optional)   DATE

A. Rules Governing *Time In* and *Time Out* of this Contract

Definition of Time In: "Time In" refers to the period of time the girl is subject to terms and conditions of this contract. *Time In* is to be considered in effect at all times when the girl is in the Mistress's presence or communicating with her in any way.

Definition of Time Out: "Time Out" refers to specific periods of time when the girl is **not** subject to the terms and conditions of this contract. The following rules apply to this *"Time Out"* period:

1. Mistress may call a "Time Out" any time She wishes.

2. (This "Time out" can be for a specific period of time or an open-ended period of time.)

3. The girl may request a "Time Out" for a specific period of time only. The girl must state her reasons and the time period for the request and await her Mistress's permission for the Time Out. Should her Mistress not grant the Time Out, her only option is to end her current relationship with her Mistress.

B. Mistress/slave Dynamics (*Written from the perspective of the slave*) *(Make changes by (1) crossing out the rule and writing into the contract its substitute in the blank space at the end of this section or (2) just crossing out the wording and writing in the new word or words above or below it. (Using white-out and writing over the white-out is an alternative also.)*

1. When Mistress speaks in person or online in chat, I will stop talking or typing immediately.

2. When in private, I will **always** call Her "Mistress","Maam" or :

_____.

3. Unless not allowed to by my Mistress, in public I will put my hand around Her arm to show we are a couple. Mistress may instead want us to hold hands, do something else, or nothing at all.

4. I may not leave a conversation on the Internet or on the phone between myself and my Mistress without explaining what I need to do first and getting permission from my Mistress to leave. This is not the case if I'm cut off by the phone or Internet connection.

5. I, the slave will write down and keep on file any new rules Mistress adds to this list.

6. I will always answer immediately and sincerely every question that Mistress asks me.

7. I will always show my respect for my Mistress when in public. I want others to see how important my Mistress is to me.

When around vanilla strangers that I'll never see again it's ok to call Her (my Mistress) "Mistress" or "Maam", but around family or regular vanilla friends, I call Her by Her name. (In summary, I will address Mistress by Her name if I absolutely need to use a name; it's preferable that I use no name to address Mistress and only call Her "Mistress" or "Maam" but using Her name is okay if necessary.)

In the vanilla world, Mistress cannot require me to call Her (or someone else) in public by a title or name that would humiliate me. (I am the judge of what would humiliate me.) That can include calling Her "Mistress" in public.

8. Mistress's slave may not lie about her Mistress to others and vice versa.

9. I (the slave) am not allowed to lie *to* my Mistress or be dishonest with Her, ever. If Mistress asks me a question I will answer with complete honesty even though I think it could get me punished.

10. While with Mistress I will make a concerted effort to always look sexy for, and to act seductive with, my Mistress. My body after all is there for Her pleasure.

11. I will try to avoid looking at my Mistress's eyes straight on.

12. Sitting at the same level as my Mistress is to be avoided if possible. However in public this is difficult to.

13. Whenever I'm to be played with or otherwise taken, I will immediately take the position my Mistress orders me to be in.

14. It is my responsibility to clean off all sex toys with rubbing alcohol, soap and water after we use them.

15. I am never allowed to get out of any of my binds/shackles without permission when I'm being (or have been) tied up or shackled. The obvious exception is if there is an emergency, I am in undue pain and/or I am in some way in danger and/or in a position that puts me in danger.

16. Whenever I'm to be played with or otherwise taken, I will immediately take the position my Mistress orders (or has ordered) me to be in.

17. If I wish to say something to my Mistress that could be controversial or seem too forward, I will first ask for "*permission to speak freely*". If what I say is deemed by Mistress to be too controversial, or seem too forward, and I have not done this, I (the slave) accept that I could be punished.

18. Mistress always has the right to punish me if She thinks I deserve it.

C. What I (the slave, i.e. the girl) Will Wear *(Written from the perspective of the slave) (Make changes by (1) crossing out the rule and writing into the contract its substitute in the blank space at the end of this section or (2) just crossing out the wording and writing in the new word or words above or below it. (Using white-out and writing over the white-out is an alternative also.)*

1. Mistress has the final say on what I wear when I am with Her and that includes when we are in public and in private. In private with my Mistress I should feel uncomfortable when fully clothed. I am in essence hiding myself from Her. The exceptions to this would be if we're expecting company and/or if it's cold.

2. Mistress can decide what I'm going to wear even though we're not going to be together at that time period. What I wear however must not humiliate me or be a danger to me.

3. I am required to dress feminine and/or in role play oriented clothing at all times unless ordered not to. The exception would be if I need to dress differently for work or another public/vanilla activity of some sort.

4. Nothing loose! I will look sexy at all times. I will wear make-up. I know how important giving pleasure to my Mistress is and looking sexy gives Mistress pleasure.

5. I may *never* wear panties while in Mistress's dwelling (or our mutual home), except to take them off when entering, and in preparation to go out. Of course the exception is when I'm given permission to wear panties in the dwelling.

6. I wear dresses or skirts only unless granted permission otherwise.

7. I will make a concerted effort to procure role play outfits that my Mistress enjoys. If I have it, my schoolgirl outfit and other types of BDSM role play outfits should always be ready to wear when at my Mistress' dwelling.

8. When in private, (alone with Mistress,) if I want to put any clothing on, even a bra or panties, I will ask permission from my Mistress first.

D. Rights of the girl (the slave) *(Make changes by (1) crossing out the rule and writing into the contract its substitute in the blank space at the end of this section or (2) just crossing out the wording and writing in the new word or words above or below it. (Using white-out and writing over the white-out is an alternative also.)*

1. The girl (i.e. the slave) has the right to expect her Mistress to love, cherish and safeguard her well-being during the period of this contract.

2. The girl has the right to *privacy*. She will not be required to exhibit or provide her submissiveness and/or naked body to others unless she has given full and knowledgeable consent to her Mistress.

3. Only those who she (the slave) chooses to be made aware of this contract and/or any of its contents, will be made aware of it. This includes family, friends, business associates and neighbors.

4. The girl reserves the right to decide who may or may not be made aware of her interest in BDSM and her submission to her Mistress.

5. The girl has the right to expect her Mistress to be knowledgeable in the Dominant/submissive lifestyle and to ensure her safety and well-being while participating in any physical activity.

6. *The girl has the right to refuse to participate in any activity, at anytime, which she feels will cause her harm, jeopardize her safety or cause her emotional stress.*

7. The girl has the right to expect that the requirements of her Mistress will take into consideration her lifestyle and her business situation and adjust to them accordingly.

8. The girl has the right to ask for an adjustment or modification to the terms of this contract at any time. These adjustment(s) must be mutually agreed upon with her Mistress or the girl's only recourse is to agree to not require said adjustment(s) or modification(s) or instead to terminate the relationship with her Mistress.

9. The girl and/or her Mistress have the right to cancel this contract at any time with a simple notification to the other.

10. The girl has to right to expect her Mistress to know her, who she is and has always been, and to respect these facets of her personality and not to require her to do, or become anything which would make her uncomfortable or in any way interfere with those facets of her personality.

11. When around vanilla strangers that the girl likely never will see again, it's ok to call Her (my Mistress) "Mistress", but around family or regular vanilla friends, the girl calls Her by her name. (In summary, the girl will address Mistress by her name if she absolutely needs to use a name; it's preferable that she will use no name to address Mistress and only call her "maam" or "Mistress" but using her name is okay if necessary.)

In the vanilla world, Mistress cannot require the girl to call her, or someone else in public, by a title or name that would humiliate the girl. (The girl is the judge of what would humiliate her.) That can include calling Her "Mistress" in public.

12. The girl's Mistress may not steal from her and/or force her to commit an unlawful act.

13. Mistress may not steal from the girl and/or force the girl to commit an unlawful act.

14. Mistress's slave may not steal from her and/or force her to commit an unlawful act.

15. Mistress may not legally and/or illegally take advantage of Her slave financially.

16. Mistress's slave may not legally or illegally take advantage of Her Mistress financially.

17. Financial slavery is *never* allowed on any occasion.

E. How I (the Slave, i.e. the girl) Will Treat My Body *(Make changes by (1) crossing out the rule and writing into the contract its substitute in the blank space at the end of this section or (2) just crossing out the wording and writing in the new word or words above or below it. (Using white-out and writing over the white-out is an alternative also.)*

1. I (the slave) will always treat my body well and protect it as it exists for my Mistress's pleasure and to harm it is not only bad for me but disrespectful of my Mistress. I will need permission from my Mistress to smoke cigarettes, do drugs, eat poorly, get too little sleep and/or other dangerous activities. For Instance, if I am cooking, I am required to wear an apron to protect my body, even if Mistress is not allowing me to wear clothing at that time. *(Any Mistress that does not want her slave to protect her naked body around hot food is likely a bad Mistress and likely not a good Mistress to belong to!)*

2. At anytime if Mistress feels I am no longer the most desirable weight, She can order me to actively lose weight. I will have to go on a diet and/or workout. She can be the TaskMistress concerning this and punish me if I am not trying to lose weight or trying hard enough. Exceptions will be if I am pregnant or overweight due to a medical condition.

F. Kissing *(Make changes by (1) crossing out the rule and writing into the contract its substitute in the blank space at the end of this section or (2) just crossing out the wording and writing in the new word or words above or below it. (Using white-out and writing over the white-out is an alternative also.)*

1. Mistress may kiss me on any part of my body anytime She wishes *other than when it could embarrass or humiliate me.* If I don't want Mistress to kiss me in front of my family, co-workers or boss, etc. then Mistress is not allowed to. In private Mistress may kiss any part of my body that She wishes and at anytime and as often as She wishes.

G. Rules Affecting Me Sexually As a Slave *(Make changes by (1) crossing out the rule and writing into the contract its substitute in the blank space at the end of this section or (2) just crossing out the wording and writing in the new word or words above or below it. (Using white-out and writing over the white-out is an alternative also.)*

1. In private, Mistress may remove (or have me remove) any or all of my clothing at anytime. As a slave, when in private with your Mistress, you should feel at least somewhat uncomfortable clothed as you are hiding yourself from your Mistress.

2. When I am in bed with my Mistress, and if She is awake, I will need permission from my Mistress to leave the bed.

3. When I and my Mistress are laying down for rest or sleep, I must lay in a way in the way that She instructs me too. This is likely to better make my body available for her pleasure.

4. My pussy should *always* be kept clean and fresh when with my Mistress. After all Mistress may wish to use it for her pleasure at anytime. If Mistress checks and my pussy is not smelling and/or tasting fresh and clean then I can expect to be punished.

5. I will exercise my pussy to keep it tight for Mistress's pleasure. I can be punished if my pussy is not tight enough.

While Mistress is playing with me (or at other times), She may order me to "tighten my pussy" for a reasonable period of time. Mistress should feel the difference in pussy tightness.

My pussy being tighter than most will be a source of pride for me and Mistress will reward me for having and keeping a tight pussy!

6. When I'm being played with and at the same time Mistress orders me to cum, I will do so. I will cum longer or harder at Mistress's discretion. This called "Orgasm-on-demand" and may require some training. When I orgasm, I orgasm for my Mistress. By orgasming I show Her that I respect Her and that I know I must obey Her. As Her slave, when I'm being played with, I have no choice but to orgasm often and as hard as my Mistress orders.

7. I may not touch my Mistress's pussy, ass or breasts *ever* without Her permission.

8. Unless told otherwise, while Mistress is sexually playing with me, *I must always ask my Mistress for permission to cum* unless I have already been given permission to start my orgasm.

Also, unless told otherwise, while Mistress is sexually playing with me, *I must always ask my Mistress for permission to STOP cumming* unless I have already been given permission to stop my orgasm.

9. While Mistress is taking me (meaning making me orgasm by some means), I will orgasm especially hard when Mistress is orgasming.

10. My body exists to please my Mistress - I must always be anxious and willing to cum for my Mistress.

11. I'm not required to do this regularly but should my Mistress order me to, I will thank Her for allowing me to cum after I have orgasmed.

12. When my Mistress's hand, hands or mouth moves toward my pussy I will always instinctively spread my legs.

13. When my Mistress's hand or hands moves toward my breasts I will instinctively move my arms and stick out my chest to make my breasts as available as possible as they belong to my Mistress and are there for Her pleasure.

14. When in private, if Mistress wants any of Her friends to spank me, while clothed or in my panties, I will comply and not resist during the spanking. I have the final say if this person will spank me on my bare bottom. If the spanking is too hard and/or that person is disrespectful, I have the right to end this experience at anytime.

15. It is my decision as the slave as to whether I will rim (eat out) Mistress' or anyone else's anus.

H. *Cunningilus of the slave* *(Make changes by (1) crossing out the rule and writing into the contract its substitute in the blank space at the end of this section or (2) just crossing out the wording and writing in the new word or words above or below it. (Using white-out and writing over the white-out is an alternative also.)*

1. *Option 1*: Mistress will not eat my pussy as part of sex. <u>Mistress would only eats my pussy as a reward, or as a special occasion such as a celebration</u>. Having my pussy eaten is something I earn. When Mistress eats my pussy I will orgasm especially hard from it.

2. *Option 2*: Mistress likes my pussy juice and Her slave will be required to provide Her with as much pussy juice as She demands. When in private, at anytime, Mistress may say "pussy juice" or something like "I want pussy juice" and Her slave will quickly remove her cloths from at least her waist down and take a position where it is easiest for her Mistress to lap down her pussy juice.

As long as they're in private, *when* a slave's pussy will be played with, including eaten, is the Mistress's decision not the slave's. Her job is to keep her pussy clean and fresh and available.

If the slave is so rude as to not provide her Mistress with an adequate amount of pussy juice, (and it is her Mistress not her that will determine if it's an adequate amount), then she will have earned herself punishment. The slave's body exists to give her Mistress pleasure so refusing to do such a thing is not allowed.

I. *Cunnilingus and Pussy Worship* *(Make changes by (1) crossing out the rule and writing into the contract its substitute in the blank space at the end of this section or (2) just crossing out the wording and writing in the new word or words above or below it. (Using white-out and writing over the white-out is an alternative also.)*

1. When alone with Mistress, unless She (my Mistress) has told me to do otherwise, I am to ask to eat Her pussy every 30 minutes or so if we're playing, every 60 minutes or so if we're not. How long I will eat Her is up to Her always.

2. NO teeth ever be felt on Mistress's pussy (unless She wants it) or I'll be punished, then I will resume eating my Mistress's pussy. This can be repeated an unlimited number of times.

3. If Mistress says "**head up**" while I am eating Her, I will stop eating Her and pull my mouth off of Her pussy and wait for her next command.

4. When told to keep *my eyes down*, I will look only at Her pussy, whether She is clothed or not, until told otherwise. Mistress will say "released" or something like it, then I may raise my eyes and go about my business.

5. When I am eating Mistress's pussy it is not my decision as to when to stop but my Mistress' decision.

6. When kneeling in front of Mistress, my eyes will be on her pussy, my legs at least somewhat spread and hands on Her thighs, rubbing Her thighs sensually and with great anticipation.

7. If we are in private and I am healthy, I will always obey my Mistress's order to eat her pussy.

8. The length of time I eat Her pussy is up to Her. Literally how I eat her pussy is up to her also. If any of my body parts are in pain from this activity, I will stop and tell Mistress about it. She will them allow me to rest. *Should Mistress not allow me to rest, chances are he is a bad Mistress and I need to find another Mistress.*

9. When spending the night, or more than a couple of hours in bed with my Mistress, I may not leave the bed before asking to eat Mistress's pussy first (unless Mistress gives me permission to otherwise leave the bed.)

10. *Pussy Worship* - If I determine I have the free time in life and if Mistress okays it, I will spend perhaps hours at a time, kissing, sucking, licking, eating, looking at, touching and loving Mistress' pussy and anus. I'm doing this for relaxation so I may think of other things about my life as I do it. Mistress's pleasure is not a priority during this.

Perhaps this is best considered a form of meditation. Mistress may be watching television, resting or reading. I will be in my own little world, worshiping Mistress's pussy.

J. The Collar *(Make changes by (1) crossing out the rule and writing into the contract its substitute in the blank space at the end of this section or (2) just crossing out the wording and writing in the new word or words above or below it. (Using white-out and writing over the white-out is an alternative also.)*

1. There is the *private* collar and the *public* collar. No one needs to know that the public collar is anything more than a necklace. My public collar could be a vanilla looking necklace but the private collar would clearly be a BDSM collar meant to aid in our playtime and my submission.

2. I will wear my public collar at all times other than perhaps when showering or when I need to temporarily wear something else for a special occasion.

3. When in private, Mistress decides when I should wear my private collar versus my public collar. If Mistress has not said anything regarding this, or has not previously made a rule about it, I will continue to wear my public collar in private.

K. Spankings *(Make changes by (1) crossing out the rule and writing into the contract its substitute in the blank space at the end of this section or (2) just crossing out the wording and writing in the new word or words above or below it. (Using white-out and writing over the white-out is an alternative also.)*

A normal, good quality spanking will leave a submissive's/slave's bottom a nice shade of pink or red. This is what a slave should expect, if not hope for. If necessary however, such a spanking should be worked up to.

1. Being spanked is a very important part of my relationship with Mistress, as well as therapeutic for me as a slave. I will beg Mistress to spank me often. I will have favorite implements to be spanked by so if Mistress allows me to pick an implement to be spanked by, I will be ready to bring it (them) to Her. When ordered to I (1) will beg to be spanked and (2) afterwards I will thank Mistress, (or whoever she is having spank me,) for taking the trouble of spanking me.

2. I will without hesitation take any position my Mistress orders me to should She wish to take me, spank me or otherwise play with me or punish me. I am never allowed to block my Mistress's spanks or try to get away from a position my Mistress has ordered me to be in unless there is an emergency or I am in harm's way. Should Mistress ever spank my hand because it was blocking a blow, I will be spanked much harder and longer (*and/or be punished in other manners*) and perhaps have my hands bound in front of me, if they are not already. I will also have the humiliation of knowing I was so disrespectful.

3. If Mistress orders me to hold any of my body parts still while She is spanking me, that is what I'm required to do.

4. Whenever I and/or Mistress and I come back from being in the public, I am to ask for a "*returning from the public spanking.*" Mistress may order me to start and stop this at her will.

5. My pussy must be wet within 60 seconds into any spanking. No significant spanking will ever end at least until my pussy is wet.

6. If Mistress wishes She will train me to cum from being spanked. Most slaves can be trained to orgasm from being spanked and as a respectful slave I will learn to orgasm for my Mistress while being spanked. Within 120 seconds of the spanking starting, I will naturally start to orgasm (asking Mistress for permission to cum first of course). Also Mistress can instead *order me* to start my orgasm during the spanking at anytime 120 seconds or longer into the spanking. As always I will need permission to *stop* my orgasm, assuming I am still being spanked.

For training me to cum from being spanked, Mistress will likely start by using a vibrator on me during the spanking and ordering me to start orgasming just as he starts the vibrator that's on my clitoris.

Mistress acknowledges that I may need up to 10 training sessions with a vibrator in this manner. After then, should I disrespect my Mistress by not cumming while being spanked, (assuming I was given permission to cum,) then I will be punished.

7. During a spanking I may never try to block the blows or try to leave the position She has put me in. When I'm being bound or shackled I *will not* resist, however when I am being bound I may always tell my Mistress that it hurts in an unacceptable manner (if it hurts) so She can make any necessary changes.

8. Whenever I am to leave the house (apartment or where ever) for more than just quickly going to the car, or something quick of that nature, whether I'm also leaving with Mistress or not, I will ask my Mistress for a "going out in the public spanking." This is over and above any other spankings I may have recently received. Mistress may order me to start and stop this at her will.

9. When alone with Mistress, unless She has told me to do otherwise, I am to ask every hour, at the beginning of the hour, to be spanked for "my hourly spanking," no matter whether I've been spanked recently or not. Mistress may not want to spank me but I'm required to ask roughly on the start of each hour anyway. Mistress may order me to start and stop this at her will.

10. Any crying I do while being spanked (if I need to cry at all) will simply be a turn on for my Mistress and will not affect the length or to an extent, intensity of my punishment. If I cry while being punished it likely means I'm learning my lesson and am getting what I deserved. The exception is when I'm experiencing physical pain from other correctable sources. For instances if my hands are tied and my shoulder is in a painful position, I should always feel free to tell Mistress about that and Mistress is obligated to immediately take me out of the situation that caused me that pain. Reasonable pain from being spanked however is not something that can be negotiated (*assuming this point has been agreed upon by both parties*.) If I do not like the kind of pain my Mistress ever gives me directly from being spanked, I need to find another Mistress or leave the BDSM lifestyle.

11. The duration and intensity of a spanking and what my Mistress uses on my bottom is always the choice of my Mistress. I may however discuss something that concerns me at anytime regarding this.

12. When Mistress and I are together, if I feel that I am getting into a bad mood, I'm to immediately ask for a "mood correction spanking" from my Mistress. This rule is repeated every five minutes until the mood changes. Should Mistress think I need yet another mood correction spanking and I fail to ask for another spanking within 5 minutes, I will receive a caning instead, and/or be put in the corner and/or be put in a cage and/or be tied/shackled alone somewhere else.

13. No blood or blisters from being spanked or otherwise beaten. If something of that nature occurs by accident it can be forgiven by the slave if she wishes. It also depends on how fragile the slave's body is.

14. I must give my okay for Mistress to spank me anywhere other than my buttocks. (See separate rules concerning flogging my breasts.) I acknowledge that sometimes my upper legs will get spanked as well as my buttocks and I give my okay to that.

L. Foreplay *(Make changes by (1) crossing out the rule and writing into the contract its substitute in the blank space at the end of this section or (2) just crossing out the wording and writing in the new word or words above or below it. (Using white-out and writing over the white-out is an alternative also.)*

1. As She prepares to take me or otherwise have me for Her pleasure, Mistress determines what our foreplay will be. I am allowed to make suggestions as to what to include in foreplay and always allowed to tell Mistress if something makes me uncomfortable or hurts.

Mistress might like me to kneel naked on the floor by the bed, chair or couch in preparation for me being taken or otherwise played with. I'll remove Her clothing when ordered to, climb on the bed and give Mistress a massage, including a butt massage. Again Mistress determines what part of Her I massage and how long I massage any part of Her.

Mistress may then turn over and I will turn my attention to Mistress's beautiful pussy when ordered to.

M. Miscellaneous Physical (including sexual) Orders I (the girl, i.e. the slave) Will Obey *(Make changes by (1) crossing out the rule and writing into the contract its substitute in the blank space at the end of this section or (2) just crossing out the wording and writing in the new word or words above or below it. (Using white-out and writing over the white-out is an alternative also.)*

1. When I am laying on my stomach for any reason and my Mistress says "elbows", I am to raise my upper body up on my elbows so my breasts are readily available to my Mistress to reach under my torso and play with. My elbows must not block access to my breasts. My breasts after all are my Mistress's property.

2. If I am kneeling or sitting on a hard surface, including a carpeted surface, Mistress will make sure I am on a lot of padding.

3. When I am crawling, perhaps while being lead naked by a leash, I will mainly be crawling on padded surfaces (such as carpeting) so as to not harm myself. Crawling on the floor for a short distance is okay.

4. While with Mistress, if my Mistress ever says "kneel in front of the bed", unless She points out a particular spot to kneel at, I am to automatically assume I am to immediately go to the pad on the floor next to the bed and kneel on it waiting for his further instructions. My eyes are to be looking down on the bed and staying that way until Mistress releases me.

If Mistress just says "kneel" I will kneel in front of Her wherever She is and wait for Her next instructions. My eyes will be on Her pussy (or Her clothed midsection) as I hope to be eating it soon.

N. Anal Sex *(Make changes by (1) crossing out the rule and writing into the contract its substitute in the blank space at the end of this section or (2) just crossing out the wording and writing in the new word or words above or below it. (Using white-out and writing over the white-out is an alternative also.)*

1. Once I have given my Mistress permission in our relationship to take me anally *at anytime*, She may at anytime take me or otherwise play with me anally (after I'm lubed up real well).

Has the slave given such permission now?

Yes_____ (if so the slave must initial it): _____

2. I have the right at anytime to require Mistress to put more lubrication in my anus and/or on Her finger, fist or toys she'll use in me, if I feel there is not enough lubrication. Mistress may never re-enter my pussy with something after entering my anus with that thing, prior to it being cleaned very well, as infections can occur that way.

3. As just noted, Mistress may insert toys into my anus as She plays with me but no toy touching my anus may be used for any other purpose until I have cleaned it thoroughly with rubbing alcohol, soap and water.

4. Mistress may insert a (finger for finger-fucking) into my anus if his finger nail is well manicured and clipped, lubricated and it will not harm my anus.

O. Pussy unshaved, unshaven and if unshaved, it's appearance *(Make changes by (1) crossing out the rule and writing into the contract its substitute in the blank space at the end of this section or (2) just crossing out the wording and writing in the new word or words above or below it. (Using white-out and writing over the white-out is an alternative also.)*

1. It is Mistress's decision on whether Her slave's pussy is shaved or unshaved, trimmed or untrimmed and if trimmed to what extent and what the design is. The slave has final say in regard to any waxing.

2. I will keep the area by my pussy clean and shaven as per my Mistress instructions.

P. Play Rape (*Make changes by (1) crossing out the rule and writing into the contract its substitute in the blank space at the end of this section or (2) just crossing out the wording and writing in the new word or words above or below it. (Using white-out and writing over the white-out is an alternative also.)*

1. I hereby give Mistress permission to include *Play Rape* at any point during our playtimes. I will not resist unless ordered to as that could give Mistress the wrong impression as to if I'm enjoying it or not it. I likely will also be bound as She takes me. I may be allowed to resist only from the waist up.

Q. Breast Bondage & Related (*Make changes by (1) crossing out the rule and writing into the contract its substitute in the blank space at the end of this section or (2) just crossing out the wording and writing in the new word or words above or below it. (Using white-out and writing over the white-out is an alternative also.)*

1. In private Mistress has access to my breasts at anytime. I will take whatever position Mistress orders me to so as to make my breasts more easily and readily accessible to Her.

2. When Mistress flogs my breasts I expect my nipples to become erect, my breasts to perhaps become some shade of red and tender if flogged for a lengthy period. I understand that flogging my breasts may become an integral part of our playtime. *I have the final say as to what Mistress can spank my breasts with and how long my breasts are spanked.*

No blood or blisters. Unless I bruise easily (which often also means the bruises go away quickly also,) bruising is to be avoided with any playtime activity.

3. Mistress may use my breasts for safe breast bondage.

4. If I allow it, Mistress may drip melted wax on my naked breasts as I am tied down (or in any position that She wants.)

R. Punishments *(Make changes by (1) crossing out the rule and writing into the contract its substitute in the blank space at the end of this section or (2) just crossing out the wording and writing in the new word or words above or below it. (Using white-out and writing over the white-out is an alternative also.)*

As previously noted, Mistress always has the right to punish me if She thinks I deserve it.

A list of ways Mistress can punish me can be added here.

S. *Medical Play* *(Make changes by (1) crossing out the rule and writing into the contract its substitute in the blank space at the end of this section or (2) just crossing out the wording and writing in the new word or words above or below it. (Using white-out and writing over the white-out is an alternative also.)*

Safe medical scenes/gyno play utilizing the slave as the patient is allowed whenever the Mistress wants it but the slave has the final say on what can be done to her.

T. *Showering and Bathing* *(Make changes by (1) crossing out the rule and writing into the contract its substitute in the blank space at the end of this section or (2) just crossing out the wording and writing in the new word or words above or below it. (Using white-out and writing over the white-out is an alternative also.)*

1. Mistress may order me to shower or take a bath *at anytime* that She wishes. I will smell fresh and clean from it or be punished.

2. Mistress may order me to shower or bath *with her* at anytime that She wishes. Mistress may bath me as She wishes, assuming it does not put me in danger.

3. I cannot be ordered by Mistress to bath naked with another person if I don't want to. Mistress may order me to bath him or her while I am clothed though. I don't need to touch their private parts if I don't want to.

4. If I am bathing or showering with Mistress, She has the right to require me to scrub him or otherwise bath Her and/or play with Her as to her specifications.

U. Massaging Mistress *(Make changes by (1) crossing out the rule and writing into the contract its substitute in the blank space at the end of this section or (2) just crossing out the wording and writing in the new word or words above or below it. (Using white-out and writing over the white-out is an alternative also.)*

1. If in private, at anytime, Mistress can order me to massage Her in wherever way She wishes. Mistress determines the length of the massage, its intensity, what body parts I massage and what I'll be wearing (or not wearing) while massaging. I might be giving Mistress long breast and butt massages!

V. Corner Time *(Make changes by (1) crossing out the rule and writing into the contract its substitute in the blank space at the end of this section or (2) just crossing out the wording and writing in the new word or words above or below it. (Using white-out and writing over the white-out is an alternative also.)*

1. When my Mistress requires me to do corner time, I will be positioned in the corner, naked, unless otherwise decided by my Mistress. I will go there immediately without resisting.

If possible my hands may be tied together to the ceiling above my head, and my legs may be tied to a leg spreader bar. I may or may not be spanked during corner time and I may or may not be required to cum (from the use of dildos, fingers or vibrators on me) for my Mistress during corner time. My Mistress will determine how long my corner time is and how often I am to be spanked while there and how often I will be required to cum, if at all.

If I need to go to the bathroom or have physical problems, Mistress is required to release me from cornertime to satisfy those problems. I then can be returned to cornertime if Mistress wishes.

W. Pulling Out Individual Pubic Hairs as Punishment *(Make changes by (1) crossing out the rule and writing into the contract its substitute in the blank space at the end of this section or (2) just crossing out the wording and writing in the new word or words above or below it. (Using white-out and writing over the white-out is an alternative also.)*

1. As punishment, if I allow it, Mistress, using a tweezers and magnifying glass, can pull out individual pubic hairs. I may or may not be tied down for this punishment.

X. Unacceptable Behavior of the slave which includes Jealousy, Pouting, Being Bitchy, Slovenly and Lazy *(Make changes by (1) crossing out the rule and writing into the contract its substitute in the blank space at the end of this section or (2) just crossing out the wording and writing in the new word or words above or below it. (Using white-out and writing over the white-out is an alternative also.)*

1. Acting in the above manner will be a recipe for punishment.

Y. *Mistress Having Multiple Slaves* (Make changes by (1) crossing out the rule and writing into the contract its substitute in the blank space at the end of this section or (2) just crossing out the wording and writing in the new word or words above or below it. (Using white-out and writing over the white-out is an alternative also.)

1. If I agree to it, Mistress may have one or more additional female and male slaves, of which I am one.

2. Once I agree to it, when in private, Mistress can order me to play with her other slave(s) in the manner that She wishes. Mistress can also play/have sex with us all at the same time (and separately) if the proper sanitation and contraceptive precautions are being adhered to.

3. I will not be jealous of the attention the other slave(s) gets which includes Mistress' sexual favors. I will expect to be punished if I get jealous of Mistress giving Her other slave(s) attention.

4. If I am playing with the other slave I will take her/his pleasure and needs very seriously, as she/he is also required to do with me.

5. All of Mistress's slaves will need permission to play with each other. Sometimes I will be the dominant person when playing with the other slave and vice versa. That will be Mistress' decision.

6. If She requires it, Mistress might require that a slave ask Her permission before using a blindfold, gag and/or other play toys on another of her slaves during slave-slave play.

7. I will care about my Mistress' other slave(s) life as well as my Mistress'.

Z. Having Sex and playing with Others Besides Mistress *(Make changes by (1) crossing out the rule and writing into the contract its substitute in the blank space at the end of this section or (2) just crossing out the wording and writing in the new word or words above or below it. (Using white-out and writing over the white-out is an alternative also.)*

If I allow it, others at my Mistress's discretion may kiss me, touch and/or otherwise play with my sexual private parts as my Mistress sees fit. If I allow it, Mistress *may* order me to suck on somebody's cock, eat their pussy, have intercourse with them, make out with them, kiss them and/or bath them.

If I allow it, others at my Mistress's discretion may use me for purposes of BDSM play.

AA. Objectification (Objectification is requiring the slave to act like an object, such as a footstool.) *(Make changes by (1) crossing out the rule and writing into the contract its substitute in the blank space at the end of this section or (2) just crossing out the wording and writing in the new word or words above or below it. (Using white-out and writing over the white-out is an alternative also.)*

If both parties agree to it, provide more specifics here:

BB. Mummification (full plastic wrap) (This is the wrapping of the slave's body in plastic film [Saran Wrap type] from below the neck down to as far as the toes.) *(Make changes by (1) crossing out the rule and writing into the contract its substitute in the blank space at the end of this section or (2) just crossing out the wording and writing in the new word or words above or below it. (Using white-out and writing over the white-out is an alternative also.)*

Mummification of the slave from her shoulders down is allows at her Mistress's discretion.

CC. Blind Folds *(Make changes by (1) crossing out the rule and writing into the contract its substitute in the blank space at the end of this section or (2) just crossing out the wording and writing in the new word or words above or below it. (Using white-out and writing over the white-out is an alternative also.)*

The use of a blindfold on the slave by her Mistress can be done on any occasion if the slave doesn't object.

DD. Pin Wheel Use *(Make changes by (1) crossing out the rule and writing into the contract its substitute in the blank space at the end of this section or (2) just crossing out the wording and writing in the new word or words above or below it. (Using white-out and writing over the white-out is an alternative also.)*

Judicial use of the Wattenberg wheel (Pin Wheel) use on the slave's is allowed except for the following areas of her body:

a) anywhere in/on her pussy,

b) anywhere from the neck up,

c) her knees

d) on her anus

e)

f)

G)

EE. Crossplaying (Crossplaying is where the slave is bound naked (or otherwise) to a large wooden cross and the Mistress does with her as She wishes.) *(Make changes by (1) crossing out the rule and writing into the contract its substitute in the blank space at the end of this section or (2) just crossing out the wording and writing in the new word or words above or below it. (Using white-out and writing over the white-out is an alternative also.)*

Safe crossplaying is allowed as Mistress desires it.

FF. *Orgasm Denial* *(Make changes by (1) crossing out the rule and writing into the contract its substitute in the blank space at the end of this section or (2) just crossing out the wording and writing in the new word or words above or below it. (Using white-out and writing over the white-out is an alternative also.)*

Orgasm Denial of Her slave is allowed to be done periodically by her Mistress.

GG. *Maid Service* *(Make changes by (1) crossing out the rule and writing into the contract its substitute in the blank space at the end of this section or (2) just crossing out the wording and writing in the new word or words above or below it. (Using white-out and writing over the white-out is an alternative also.)*

Maid service will be provided at least semi-regularly by the slave if her Mistress wants it.

HH. *Gags* *(Make changes by (1) crossing out the rule and writing into the contract its substitute in the blank space at the end of this section or (2) just crossing out the wording and writing in the new word or words above or below it. (Using white-out and writing over the white-out is an alternative also.)*

Mistress may use a gag on Her slave. Her slave however has the right to not allow isolated instances of it.

II. *Strap-on Dildos & Vibrators (Make changes by (1) crossing out the rule and writing into the contract its substitute in the blank space at the end of this section or (2) just crossing out the wording and writing in the new word or words above or below it. (Using white-out and writing over the white-out is an alternative also.)*

Use of strap-on dildos and vibrators **are allowed** on the slave when taking the slave in her pussy and ass.

When and how often these are used on the slave is the Mistress' decision.

If the strap-on touches or enters an anus, it may not be used on the slave in any way until it is thoroughly cleaned off as it is no longer sanitary anymore.

JJ. *Mistress Being Taken with a Dildo/vibrator (Make changes by (1) crossing out the rule and writing into the contract its substitute in the blank space at the end of this section or (2) just crossing out the wording and writing in the new word or words above or below it. (Using white-out and writing over the white-out is an alternative also.)*

If Mistress wishes it, Her slave(s) **will** use a strap-on or vibrator to play with and/or have intercourse in her Mistress.

KK. *Handcuffs, Chains and Shackles* *(Make changes by (1) crossing out the rule and writing into the contract its substitute in the blank space at the end of this section or (2) just crossing out the wording and writing in the new word or words above or below it. (Using white-out and writing over the white-out is an alternative also.)*

Handcuffing, chaining and shackling of the slave for purposes of bondage **is** allowed if done safely and in private. If not in private, the slave must okay it on each occurrence.

LL. *Leather, Rubber or Latex Clothing* *(Make changes by (1) crossing out the rule and writing into the contract its substitute in the blank space at the end of this section or (2) just crossing out the wording and writing in the new word or words above or below it. (Using white-out and writing over the white-out is an alternative also.)*

1. Mistress may require her slave to wear leather, rubber and/or latex clothing.

MM. *Role Playing* *(Make changes by (1) crossing out the rule and writing into the contract its substitute in the blank space at the end of this section or (2) just crossing out the wording and writing in the new word or words above or below it. (Using white-out and writing over the white-out is an alternative also.)*

Role playing (RP) is allowed. Allowable role playing scenarios are to be written in below. When the role playing will begin is always at the Mistress's discretion. (*Any additional RP scenarios can be added at later times with both parties signing and dating the additions.*)

1. When in private with her Mistress, and in a safe and private environment, and at her Mistress's discretion, the slave is required to wear any role play outfit Mistress wants her to (and that is available to them.) This includes school girl outfits, nursing uniform, etc.

2. Mistress will always have the final word as to how the role play outfit is worn.

Role Play Scenarios

A)

B)

C)

D)

E)

NN. *Cumming From Performing Cunnilingus on Mistress* *(Make changes by (1) crossing out the rule and writing into the contract its substitute in the blank space at the end of this section or (2) just crossing out the wording and writing in the new word or words above or below it. (Using white-out and writing over the white-out is an alternative also.)*

1. If Mistress requires it, Her slave will train herself to orgasm from just performing cunnilingus on her Mistress. Mistress must give her an adequate training period, including using a vibrator on her while she is performing cunnilingus but at some point if the slave is not cumming from giving her Mistress cunnilingus alone, she should expect to be punished.

OO. *Birth Control* *(Make changes by (1) crossing out the rule and writing into the contract its substitute in the blank space at the end of this section or (2) just crossing out the wording and writing in the new word or words above or below it. (Using white-out and writing over the white-out is an alternative also.)*

1. The slave promises to actively and aggressively guard her body from unwanted pregnancy.

PP. Tattoos, Branding, Piercing (*Make changes by (1) crossing out the rule and writing into the contract its substitute in the blank space at the end of this section or (2) just crossing out the wording and writing in the new word or words above or below it. (Using white-out and writing over the white-out is an alternative also.)*)

1. I the slave will always have the final decision on whether I am going to have on my body any tattoos, branding, piercing or any other type of semi-permanent or permanent physical alterations. However, if I want to do any of the previously mentioned, *but* my Mistress doesn't want me to do it, then I am not allowed to do it. Thus if I want to have a piercing but my Mistress won't allow it, I will not be able to get that piercing.

SS. *None of the below activities are allowed without the consent (on each occasion) of both parties:*

Erotic Dance
Defilement,
Seeing a Partner Dirty or Wet
Exhibitionism/Sex in Public
Furry
Hair Pulling
High Heels
Hunt-and-Capture
Lace/Lingerie
Leather
Making Home
Masks
Podophilia (Foot Fetish)
Sissification
Urolagnia (Water Sports/Urine)
Voyeurism
Tickling
Blood play
Knife play
Breath control (breathplay, asphyxiation)
Scat play
Urine play
Collar and Lead/Leash
Tit shocking
Hypnosis of the submissive
Forced cross-dressing
Forced homosexuality or bi-sexuality of the submissive
Nipple torture
Spitting on the submissive
Toilet play

Diaper play (Master's submissive may not be required to wear a diaper.)
Needle play
Electric Play (*Tens, Violet Wand and Shock devices*)
CBT (cock and ball torture)
Boot worship by the submissive of her Master's boots
Kissing of clean boots/shoes of others
Verbal abuse
Ashtray play (When the submissive makes herself like a table so her Master can put an ashtray on her back.)
Forced chastity
Sensory deprivation
Suspension/suspension play
Humiliation
Daddy/daughter
Forced 24/7 servitude of the submissive.
Public exhibition of a submissive
Pain enhancement of the submissive
Ponygirl play (where the submissives pretends to be a pony, is dressed up as such and ridden.)
Duct tape use on the submissive
Purposely stretching of any part of the submissive's body
Forced confinement of the submissive
Total Power Exchange (TPE) - (TPE is loosely defined as one person [the Master] completely, utterly and totally making the decisions for himself and his submissive.)
Unusual mind control games
Rimming (licking, eating, and/or otherwise using the mouth/tongue on/in her Master's anus).
Fisting of the submissive's pussy
Fisting of the submissive's anus
Pantyhose/Stockings
Participating in Erotic Photography
Pinching
Pussy-Whipping
Tit-shocking
Bestiality (This is illegal. Don't do it.)

ADDITIONAL RULES

Other BDSM Books by Phil G. Include:

*BDSM Master/slave Contract
*The Absolutely Essential Book of BDSM and S&M Rules
*Things To Do During 3 Hours of Sex; A Step-by-step Guide
*Playtime At The Dom Den; A Step-by-step Guide
*The Absolutely Essential Guide to Great BDSM and S&M Sex
*The Absolutely Essential Dominant/submissive Playtime Experience
*The Absolutely Essential BDSM Sexual Experience
*The Ultimate Collection of S&M and BDSM Rules For Female Submissives and Slaves
*Master and submissive or slave BDSM Contract
*The Funniest BDSM Personal Ads
*Have Awesome BDSM Sex
*The Spanking Dictionary
*Spanking Contract
*BDSM Rules
*Bed Arrest, the Punishment for BDSM Enthusiasts
*Dramatic Weight Loss Using BDSM

The Spanking Dictionary

The Spanking Dictionary

By Phil G.

ISBN-13: 978-1492228486
ISBN-10: 1492228486

Erotic BDSM Books - Your Erotic BDSM Book Publisher
EroticBDSMbooks.com

The Spanking Dictionary

Caution is always advised in anything related to spanking, discipline and punishment. Always stay within legal boundaries.

Spanking pronouns, (which include names of spanking websites, spanking actors/actresses, spanking parties and spanking media) are NOT included in this dictionary due to space limitations. **Spanking of minors is not discussed in this book nor advocated**.

ADULT SPANKING - Spanking taking place among and between people who are of legal age.

ADULT SPANKING SCENARIOS - Spanking activities that take place among adults. These are often thought up and set up ahead of time.

AMATEUR SPANKING – (1) Unless a person is spanking, or receiving spankings for money or other material gain (such as Spanking Therapists and professional FemDoms do,) then this category includes most in the adult spanking world. (2) While not all agree on this angle of the definition, it has been used to imply a spanker or spankee who is not proficient in the spanking arts.

ANAL EXAM – The dominant spends a lot of time inspecting, testing and ultimately using the spankee's anus for his/her pleasure.

ANGER MANAGEMENT THERAPY SPANKING - Spanking can be used as a kind of therapy to help manage anger. There are two different approaches.

(1) The angered/stressed person is the *spankee* and gets spanked for a length and an intensity that allows the anger/stress to be released. Multiple spankings may be needed.

(2) The angered/stressed person is the *spanker* and spanks for a length and an intensity that allows the anger/stress to be released. Multiple spankings may be needed.

ANNIVERSARY SPANKING - Like birthday spankings this involves a tradition where as part of the festivities one or multiple participants spank and/or get spanked. It may include a special sexual scenario also. Spankophiles might want to get creative and have these anniversaries occur on other anniversaries such as when the couple met, became engaged and/or had their first date.

AVERAGE SPANKING (An) – Your basic everyday spanking, the usual. (Yawn.)

BARE BOTTOM SPANKINGS – Applying the spanking directly to the uncovered buttocks.
There are advantages to this versus spanking the covered buttocks:

1) *Better access*; the spanker may wish to use the spankee's bottom for other types of stimulation including anal and vaginal stimulation. The spanker may want to rub the naked bottom sensually at various times, etc.

2) *Humiliation*; the spankee must expose him/herself.

3) *Intensity*; clothing can lessen the impact of the blows and thus lessen the spanking's sensation and/or ability to provide punishment.

4) *Safety*; All parties can see how the buttocks is fairing from the blows. Perhaps the intensity needs to be lessened; you might not know if the buttocks are covered.

BARE BOTTOM BEATING – See *Bare Bottom Spankings*.

BATHBRUSH – A long handled brush used for washing one's self during bathing. It can be an effective spanking tool.

BEDROOM TIME – Being banished to the bedroom after, and/or as part of a punishment spanking. Often this bad girl will get spanked more than once while serving bedroom time.

BED ARREST – A type of BDSM punishment. See "*Bed Arrest, the Punishment for BDSM Enthusiasts*".

BEDTIME SPANKING – (1) Spankings irregularly administered as foreplay to sex prior to going to sleep for the night. (2) Spankings which are administered nightly (or irregularly) when the spankee and/or spanker goes to bed, whether there is to be sexual activity or not.

A number of spankees claim a bedtime spanking helps make them sleepy.

BEHAVIOR MODIFICATION SPANKING – Spanking(s) administered to change unwanted behavior. Repeated and hard spankings may well be necessary to make this work.

BELT – It holds a man's pants up and is a nasty spanking implement. You're in for it now young lady!

BIRCHING – Birching is to spank using a tied together collection of thin tree switches. A nice touch is to have the spankee go out and pick the tree switches herself and tie them together securely for future use or use as soon as it is made.

BIRTHDAY SPANKING - A "traditional" birthday spanking is given on the birthday of the spankee. The formula is to administer one swat for each year of age, plus one additional swat "to grow on, one to live on, one to be happy on, to get married on, etc." The last swat can be the hardest as it's for any bad behavior that he/she did last year.

Spankee beware! Many will say that each birthday party attendee gets to give the same number of spanks, which can make for hundreds of spanks!

The spankee might pick and choose who gets to do the spanking and birthday spankings are typically done clothed as it's often done at children's parties.
Birthday spankings are usually done by hand but if it involves consenting adults spanking that often won't be the case.

Dominants may want to incorporate "practice birthday spankings" with their submissives as another excuse to spank.

Birthday spankings can be given belatedly but typically are for only the spankee's previous birthday (not all his/her birthdays.)

Blindfolding the adult spankee might be a nice touch.

A "*Reverse Birthday Spanking*" is when the person having the birthday gets to give the spankings instead!

BOARD OF CORRECTION – Slang name for a paddle.

BOTTOMS UP – While more known as a saying for drinking everything from a glass (container) so the bottom of the container is pointing up (thus sending all the liquid into your mouth,) this also means presenting a bottom for a spanking.

BOTTOM RAKING - Sliding your fingernails over and across the spanked or unspanked ass. This should not be done hard enough to puncture the skin or even take any layers of skin off. This should also only be done over the fleshy part of the buttocks and not near the anus or sexual organs.

BROKE THE PADDLE ON MY BUTT – This saying can be put in different ways. It's a source of pride for the spankee that when someone spanked his/her butt using a paddle, the paddle broke upon hitting his/her butt.

BRUTAL SPANKING – See *Severe Spanking*.

CAPSAICIN CREAM – (Results vary from individual to individual.) - Applying a *very small* amount of this cream onto the naked buttocks is an alternative to spanking (thus is called "*Silent Spanking*"). It seeps into the bottom and often is painful. A surprisingly small amount is needed. Make sure to quickly wash your hands after applying it or you will be in pain too. (Better yet use something else to apply it with.)

Rub the *capsaicin cream* in well. It might take some time to make its impact well noticed. Spankers I suggest you first experiment by rubbing a tiny bit into your spankee's butt. Only drops of it would be necessary to first test his/her resistance to it. Olive oil or vegetable oil can help dissipate the pain. This cream may look innocent but the stuff is *evil*! (Tiger Balm is another possible punishment cream.) Do not put any of this on or in the anus or vagina!

CANING – This is when a cane is applied with force to the buttocks of the spankee. The cane can hurt more than many other spanking implements due to its smaller surface area so caution is advised. Also see *Switching*.

CARPET BEATER – A long handled housekeeping tool used to beat dust off of hanging rugs and to spank worthy bottoms.

CHARITY SPANKING - Charity Spanking is when people are spanked in exchange for others sponsoring them and giving money to one or more charities for each good spank they take. Also see *Professional Spanking*.

CLENCHING – (Clenching Cheeks) – This is when the spankee tightens his/her buttocks muscles together forcefully. This might be done in an attempt to dull the sting of the spanking.

COMING BACK IN FROM THE PUBLIC SPANKINGS – After the spankee returns to a private secluded setting, after having been in the public (and that includes having been to work or having been shopping), she gets a spanking as a natural course of events. This is over and above any other spankings she's getting for any other reason. This is associated with but the opposite of *Going Out in the Public Spanking*.

CONFESSIONAL {THERAPY} SPANKING - (1) A religiously related spanking scene where the spanker plays an authoritative person of religious faith who spanks the spankee in an effort to get him/her to be more religiously righteous or pay for his/her sins. This may be more popular in Domestic Discipline households. (This happened for real a lot more in centuries past than most hear about.)

(2) The spankee perhaps was raised in a strict religious environment and needs that type of strict (and perhaps regular) guidance to stay on the straight and narrow. A good spanking once or twice a week for just this could be a pleasant addition to your relationship. This obviously has similarities to the confessional of Catholics and doing penance.

(3) In an attempt to get the spankee to confess to something, he/she is spanked. Once he/she confesses then punishment would be administered, which would be another type of spanking such as *Punishment Spanking*.

CONFIDENTIAL SPANKING – The spanking partners agree to keep their spanking relationship and other spanking related activities secret, except to whom they both agree on. It is essential to follow this rule.

CONSENSUAL SPANKING – Informed and agreed-upon spanking that takes place between and among consenting adults.

CORPORAL PUNISHMENT – This is physical punishment inflicted on the human body. This includes spanking but can also include the death penalty.

CROP – A slapping instrument originally meant to urge horses to move. It can be a wonderful spanking implement.

CRUEL TO BE KIND – A saying that is loosely associated with the potentially beneficial impact of adult spanking.

DETENTION ROOM – This is where many naughty schoolgirls go in spanking films and fantasies. This is the location of much discipline, primarily spanking.

DISCIPLINE - It incorporates punishment to correct disobedience of the rules and/or other unacceptable behavior.

DIZZY SPANKING - For this kind of spanking, the spankee is spun around on foot or in a chair that can spin around, until he/she is dizzy. The spankee is then spanked. This is for healthy spankees only and it's essential to take care for safety.

DOMESTIC DISCIPLINE – (*Christian Domestic Discipline, Spanking for Jesus, Loving Domestic Discipline*) – This typically is discipline relegated for couples, and often is administered in Christian dominated households. Rules are instituted and penalties for disobedience are administered. The male tends to be the dominate person (*Head of Household* [HOH]).

DOMINATION SPANKING – The spanking often includes additional aspects of domination such as oral commands, punishment and physical restraint.

DROPSEAT PAJAMAS – These pajamas open at the buttocks for excreting waste and spanking.

DUEL SPANKING - (*Tandem Spanking*) - This is a *Spanking Contest* between spanking couples. The spanking is done simultaneous or one at a time. See *Spanking Contest*.

ENDURANCE SPANKING - This can be done to determine the spanking length and intensity limits of a spankee. (Of course limits change with time.) How much can the spankee take, how many swats, how hard can the swats be, how long can the spanking go on? Are there certain spanking implements that the spankee doesn't do as well with?

Spanking models often go through this unless they have good references.

ENEMA SPANKINGS – Combining enemas with spankings. The spankee is given a spanking then an enema is administered. The spankee releases the water and immediately gets another spanking.

EROTIC SPANKING - Erotic Spanking are spanking activities and techniques that are executed expressly to enhance sexual pleasure. Admittedly spanking (even the thought of spanking) likely enhances a spankopile's pleasure but with *Erotic Spanking* it's taken a step further. For instance the couple can alternate spankings with the use of a variety of sexual toys and/or manual sexual stimulation.

The spankee can be securely tied down so she/he is immobile and can be enjoyed in other ways after and in-between spankings.

EXERCISE SPANKING – If the spankee needs motivation to exercise and/or exercise harder, spanking can be of use. The spankee can be spanked whenever exercise goals are not reached and/or can get the more desirable reward of a pleasurable spanking when the goals are met.

EXHIBITION SPANKING – This is when spanking models, professional or amateur, provide the public with a spanking related show. The spankee(s) could be clothed or exposed. Also see *Public Spanking*.

EXORCISM SPANKING – ("Exorcism Beating") - This occurred historically in various places and times in both western and eastern orthodox Christianity, as well as in other religions. This also occurred as part of the inquisitions. In most cases however, the spankee was lucky if their main punishment was only being spanked (beaten.)

Over the centuries some clergy members, particularly those that still were allowed to have sex, set up chambers where women were spanked, sometimes on a sizable wooden cross, for their purported transgressions. It might have been just one spanking or a semi-regular occurrence.

The spankee's buttocks may or may not be exposed for the beating and onlookers may or may not be allowed to watch, or even aid in the beatings.

F/f SPANKING – Female spanking female.

F/m SPANKING - Female spanking male.

FIFTY SHADES OF GREY - A groundbreaking, famous 2011 erotic romance novel by British author E. L. James. Its erotic scenes include BDSM activities such as bondage, discipline, dominance/submission, sadism and masochism.

FIRM HAND – The spanker has a strong and likely big hand that can deliver impressively hard spanks.

FLOGGING – A flogger is a variation of the cat-of-nine-tails whip. It's typically made of suede or real leather and has many individual elastic strands attached to the handle.

GOING OUT IN THE PUBLIC SPANKING – Before the spankee goes out into the public (and that includes going to work or shopping), she gets a spanking as a natural course of events. This is over and above any other spankings she's getting for any other reason. This is associated with *Coming Back in from the Public Spankings*.

GOOD OLD FASHION SPANKING – These are the standard spankings we grew up with. *Silent Spankings* and many if not all spankings when the spanker is tied down to spanking furniture, likely are not in this category. This term denotes a hard or harder than normal spanking.

GROUP SPANKING – When a multiplicity of people conjugate for the expressed purposes of engaging in one or more kinds of spanking and spanking related endeavors.

HALLOWEEN SPANKING – Spanking on Halloween while people are in costume. Ideally the spankee(s) should not know who's doing the spanking. Another version has it that the spankee(s) are the ones that people can't tell the identity of.

HAIRBRUSH – (Hated Hairbrush) – The household hairbrush makes a very effective and surprisingly intense spanking tool. Mmmmmm!

HAND SPANKING – Directly applying the spanking blows to those naughty butt cheeks with your hand(s).

HANDPRINT – On a well spanked red ass, if the spanker lands a single hard spank, a white handprint on the otherwise red ass cheek might appear for a short time.

HARD SPANKINGS – A true spankophile should be able to take a hard spanking, at least from time to time. Hard spankings might only be relegated for punishment. Technically a hard spanking should not have the intensity of a severe spanking. Depending however on the pain threshold level of the spankee, a hard spanking could make a spankee cry.

Hard spankings however may evolve into your norm. You may find it best to tie down the spankee for a hard spanking.

The spanker can make demands of the spankee during a hard spanking, demands that need to be promised to be met before the spanking can stop. Perhaps by using a vibrator in her anus she would be required to cum before the spanking could stop.

Unless the spankee has very developed resistance, his/her bottom should be red and perhaps marked from a hard spanking.

If the spankee is female it's suggested that no hard spanking ever ends unless her pussy is wet just from the spanking and she's promising to be a very good girl!

HEATING PAD – (1) After a good spanking, if additional punishment is warranted, laying the heated pad over the well spanked buttocks might be the answer. (2) The spankee could place his/her butt on the heating pad before the spanking possibly making it more tender. (3) For some sitting on the heating pad can feel like punishment.

HOLIDAY SPANKING – Spankings in some cases can really add to the holiday cheer! (Of course there's always *Spanking Santa* in his red outfit!)

HOT SPANKING – Spanking that are more sexually stimulating than most.

HOUSE PADDLE – A paddle that is kept readily available as a courtesy for guests to use. (It can be another spanking implement instead and named accordingly).

HUMILIATION THERAPY SPANKING – Sometimes a person needs more humility, one way to give him or her more humility is to combine domination with long, hard spankings. Or just a long hard spanking could do the trick. Spanking Therapists and FemDoms can specialize in this.

ICE SPANKING – There are variations to this spanking technique. If you're interested you and your partner should experiment and find the way that works best for you.

The spankee will need to have her buttocks fully exposed. The spanker can do any of the following, or combine them:

a) First rub ice on/across her naked buttocks until the ice has melted. Dry the spankee's buttocks if so desired and administer a good spanking to the spankee.

b) After the first spanking is completed, start over with more ice and repeat this until you're done.

IF-THEN – This scenario can be used with adults, particularly in Domestic Discipline relationships. The number of spankings, spanking duration, intensity, length, implement used and number of spankings the spankee gets are set up ahead of time for a wide range of infractions. Over spending on a credit card would have a clear and previously defined punishment, as would being late for work etc. Couples can spend a lot of quality horny-time determining what punishments the submissive member of the relationship would get for which infraction.

IMPULSE SPANKING – Unexpectedly administering a spanking without warning and perhaps for no particular reason.

INSUFFICIENT DISCIPLINE – When the submissive party thinks (to him/herself, or out-loud) that the dominant is not disciplining him/her adequately or is strong enough emotionally to administrate the discipline.

JUICY BUTT – A bottom that likely is great for spanking (or one that someone thinks would be great for spanking.)

KNEADING (aka *Petrissage*) - The palms of the hands and/or fingers work the buttock's muscle and fat tissue. Kneading a spankee's bare buttocks is also popular before, during, and/or after a spanking.

KNICKERS DOWN – An English saying meaning "panties down" in preparation for the spanking she so desperately needs.

LEATHER BUTT - A slang term for buttocks that are comparatively insensitive to spanking and do not mark easily. With enough spankings many buttocks become less sensitive.

LESBIAN SPANKING – When women play with each other sexually, and that includes spanking.

LESBIAN SPANKING STORIES – Erotic girl-girl spanking literature.

LIMIT – The point where the submissive party is unwilling to accept any spanking related additional intensity, duration and/or experience.

LINGERIE SPANKING – Spanking while the pretty lady is wearing lingerie.

M/f SPANKING – Male spanking female.

MOTIVATIONAL SPANKING – This type of spanking scenario can help the spankee reach their goal. Perhaps the goal is good grades in college, or additional weight loss, or quitting smoking. Motivational spanking can work (but like anything in life is not guaranteed to work.)

(1) Before the spankee embarks on their endeavor he/she can be given the first motivational spanking, a hard spanking that really shows him/her that it's better to stick with the program. His/her subconscious mind needs to be motivated and a really good spanking might do just that.

(2) Should the spankee fail to reach previously established goals, he/she should be very soundly spanked and otherwise punished. Other punishments can include corner time, not being allowed to wear cloths (when in private,) Bed Arrest, orgasm denial and other forms of humiliation can also be incorporated. Perhaps you'd also like to invite all your kinky friends over to also give him/her a good spanking.

KISS OF THE PADDLE – When a blow from a paddle on the butt leaves a significant mark.

LAP-WRIGGLING SPANKING – (a.k.a. *Good Old-fashion Lap-wriggling Spanking*) – Wiggling while over a lap getting spanked. (This is more of an English term.) This wiggling likely is because the spanking is particularly intense or the spankee's ability to take a spanking is not too developed.

LIGHT SPANKING – This can be applied to a clothed or bare bottom. It can be administered by hand or via the use of a spanking implement. It should not be particularly painful for most spankees.

LONG, HARD SPANKING – A lengthy and intense punishment spanking meant to change unacceptable behavior.

MAINTENANCE SPANKINGS – (*Preventative Maintenance Spankings*) - Spankings administered on a regular basis to keep the spankee on the straight and narrow. Punishment spankings are administered in addition to these.

MARATHON SPANKING – Lengthy spanking sessions that might be part of spanking contest or simply for a couple to establish their own personal best. In some marathon spanking sessions the couple can take a short break periodically.

MARKS – (*Spanking Marks*) – A good spanking with more than moderate intensity (depending on how sensitive the spankee's bottom is) can leave the bottom a lovely shade of red. It also can leave light contusions and more significant bruises. These bruises (aka "marks") could remain for days or longer or they can be gone in hours. A spankophile is proud of these marks hence the phrase "wears her (his) marks with pride".

MEMORY RECOVERY SPANKING – Spankings administered to hopefully help the spankee remember things he/she had forgotten. The hope is that he/she can remember that forgotten thing while being spanked or afterwards.

MODERATE INTENSITY SPANKING – A spanking administered with only moderate intensity typically will give the bottom some or more redness. It shouldn't make the spankee cry or leave marks. This all depends on how sensitive the spankee's ass cheeks are.

MOTIVATIONAL SPANKING – This type of spanking scenario can help the spankee reach their goals. Perhaps the goal is good grades in college, or weight loss, or quitting smoking. Motivational spankings can work (but like anything in life is not guaranteed to work.)

(1) Before the spankee embarks on their endeavor he/she can be given the first motivational spanking, which is a serious spanking that really show him/her that it's better to stick with the program. His/her subconscious mind needs to be motivated also and a really good spanking might do just that.

(2) Should the spankee fail to reach previously established goals, he/she should be very soundly spanked and otherwise punished. Other punishments can include corner time, not being allowed to wear cloths (when in private,) Bed Arrest, orgasm denial and other forms of humiliation can also be incorporated. Perhaps you'd also like to invite all your BDSM/kinky friends over to give him/her a spanking.

MUSICAL SPANKING – Spanking to the beat of the music and/or for the length of the musical composition. (Ever spanked to "Bolero"?)

Another great thing about music is that it might cover up the sound of the spanks hitting the spankee's bottom and noises the spankee utters as his/her bottom is reddened.

NAKED SPANKING – The spankee, and optionally the spanker, are not wearing any cloths.

NSA SPANKING – (No Strings Attached Spanking) – Casual spanking where a special relationship is not necessary.

OLD FASHIONED BARE BOTTOM SPANKING – These are the standard spankings we grew up with. *Silent Spankings* and many if not all spankings when the spanker is tied down to spanking furniture, likely are not in this category. This term denotes a hard or harder than normal spanking.

OTK – (a.k.a. *OTK Spanking*) – Short for *Over The Knee*. This is one of the most popular spanking positions. Its benefits include that the spanking can start quickly versus having to tie the spankee up. Also the spankee's private parts and ass, with all its features, are in easy reach for the spanker's use (assuming the spankee allows that.)

PADDLE – A rigid spanking implement that typically is quite a bit longer than it is wide. The thickness of a paddle can vary. Paddles can increase the intensity of the spanking blows and make spanking a less tiring affair for the spankers. Paddles are usually made of wood but can be made of other hard materials such as acrylic.

PARTY SPANKING – Spanking that takes place at social gatherings. This includes *Spanking Games* and *Group Spankings*. Party Spanking is not the same as *Spanking Parties*.

PLAYFUL SPANKING – This can be when the spankee gets only light to moderate swats or a limited number of quick swats. Consensual playful spankings might be used to break the tension.

POUTING - To make a facial expression that indicates dissatisfaction; sulking. This might be done by the spankee prior to the spanking or when there is an indication that a spanking will take place in the future.

PRIVATE SPANKING - These spankings are given in an isolated private setting with invited company only.

PREVENTATIVE MAINTENANCE SPANKING – See *Maintenance Spanking*.

PROFESSIONAL SPANKING – When money or material goods are exchanged for one or more spankings. Spankings are given professionally by *Spanking Theraphists, FemDoms, Spanking Demonstrators* and others. It could also be the opposite where it's the spanking model that gets spanked in exchange for money or material goods. (This includes spanking pictures and spanking video models.) *Charity Spanking* is when people are spanked in exchange for others giving money to one or more charities for each good spank the spankee takes.

PUBLIC SPANKING – (This includes *Exhibition Spanking*) – Spankings given in a public or semi public non-group spanking environment. (Not recommended!)

PUNISHMENT AGREEMENT – A *Punishment Agreement* is an oral or written agreement that defines what punishments will be given for what offenses. See *Spanking Contract* and *BDSM Contract*.

PUNISHMENT FETISH – The idea of being punished, or even of being punished in a certain way (such as being spanked) in some way turns on the individual and could be a re-occurring fantasy.

PUNISHMENT ROOM – A room, or area of a room (often the basement, bedroom or the dominant's study) where most of the spankings take place.

PUNISHMENT SPANKING - (*Discipline Spanking*) – These spankings leave the spankee's bottom red and marked. These are hard spankings meant to change a wayward spankee's behavior. Typically the female spankee (and sometimes male) will cry from these. Also applied as part of the punishment could be corntime, bedroom time and other punishments. Perhaps the spankee will only be allowed to crawl for the rest of the day/night if going somewhere in the house, (obviously privacy is required.) Maybe one punishment spanking will not be enough, or even two! The subconscious mind needs to know what he or she did is no longer allowed!

PURIFICATION RITUAL SPANKING – This spanking category is more on the spiritual side. It can combine enemas, massage, prayer, meditation and/or bathing for spiritual arousal and/or renewal.

PUSSY SPANKING – The vagina is lightly spanked for stimulation and/or punishment.

QUICKIE SPANKING – When time is limited, but the spankee must have a spanking, he/she can be bent over the nearest applicable furniture or go over your lap for an immediate spanking. Often this is when the spankee is already dressed for an occasion. A quickie spanking needs to be given instantly, likely without any significant preparation, waiting time, discussion, or scolding.

REAL TEARS – This indicates that what's occurring is a good hard spanking! Sometimes during a spanking video shoot, the spankee, in-between takes, has a bit of water put by her eyes to mimic tears. No need to do that when the tears are real!

RED BOTTOM SPANKING - (a.k.a. *Red Ass Spanking*) – A good spanking should leave the spankee with some or more redness on his/her bottom. A bottom that is covered with redness would be from a true *Red Bottom Spanking* that the spankee can 'wear' with pride! The red bottom may be accompanied with marks (bruises).

RELIGIOUS SPANKING – Religious spanking has a very long history. Men and women's buttocks have been beaten for, and by, religious authorities in many past civilizations. Certain members of Christian clergy are recorded to have spanked (women in particular) back when it was easier for them to get away with it. Inquisitioners would beat men and women, often without mercy, as they considered them to be an affront to god.

A part of religious spanking history that may be of interest is how often women in the medieval and post medieval centuries, (often coupled women,) would request a spanking from the clergy (such as their minister or priest) as atonement for their sins or as confidential punishment for something isolated that they did. Often their husbands okayed it. Heck it was a lot better than going to hell right, at least that was what they thought.

Some church building basements had a separate section for these atonement sessions. This happened more often than people realize.

REWARD SPANKING – (1) When a spankophile just can't get enough spankings that you are actually able to reward her/him by giving a spanking. (2) A FemDom might consider all spankings she gives to her slaves to be a reward, or should be viewed as a reward. Punishment for bad behavior is typically more severe than a reward spanking.

ROMANCE SPANKING - This is for spanking couples involved in a romantic relationship. The spanking can be mixed with sexual stimulation and intercourse.

RULER – (Wooden Ruler) – Though often made of wood, it can be made of other substances. Some rulers are thicker than others and somewhat longer than one foot. The thick 1½ foot ruler is a dandy! The yardstick can be very useful for those long reaches, for instance when the naughty girl is sucking on a man's cock and he wants to spank her at the same time. (Watch out for those teeth!)

SAFE SPANKING – Don't spank too hard. Some spankees' butts are able to take more abuse than others, at least until the butt toughens up (assuming it does.) Also you want all parties to feel secure with the location and privacy of the place selected for the spanking.

SANDPAPER CHAIR – After the spankee is spanked, he or she sits naked on sandpaper. An alternative is to rub sandpaper on the spankee's well spanked bottom and/or run your fingernails over the spanked buttocks.

SCHOOLGIRL SPANKING – The naughty (adult) schoolgirl discipline fantasy is one of the most popular spanking fantasies. She is dressed in the pelted skirt and white dress shirt (perhaps also with a tie) and is constantly getting in trouble so she is constantly spanked! All female spanking enthusiasts (spankees) should have a schoolgirl outfit!

SELF-SPANKING – Spanking yourself.

SEXUAL DOMINATION – (Associated with *Sensual Domination*) - The dominant person controls and orchestrates the sexual relationship and sexual activity with the submissive person.

SERIOUS SPANKING – (1) Spanking enthusiasts that take the art of spanking seriously. (2) A hard or even severe spanking and typically is reserved for punishment.

SERVANT SPANKING – (Also see *Slave Spanking*) - Spanking of servants (though in past centuries and millennia they more often were slaves) occurred often. In those days masters and mistresses lorded over their servants with more power than they do today. If the lord (or mistress) of the house thought beating the servant would make good discipline (or simply enjoyed it), that was the servant's fate should she wish to continue working there, or often anywhere else as employment references were important.

The servant girl might be spanked for pleasure by the master of the house. She might be enjoyed in other ways too, though not as often from vaginal intercourse. Servant girls that ended up taking the role of concubines might be treated better and have less mundane work to do. Wives in those days were frigid move often than now. This might be because they were afraid to have too much sex with their husbands as it was so much easier to get pregnant back then thanks largely to a pronounced lack of birth control and the stricter demands of the prevailing religious forces that were staunchly against birth control. (Also women died during childbirth a lot more frequently back then.) A surprising number of wives simply considered the sex demands of their husbands to be too much and welcomed their use of a servant in that manner if it freed them from that arduous duty, (assuming he did not get her pregnant and kept his distance from her emotionally.)

The mistress of the house might order someone to be spanked (beaten) and perhaps do it herself. Husbands and male friends (or other servants) often were happy to do the beating for her, assuming it was a female getting spanked.

The person being beaten may or may not have the area being beaten, fully exposed (thus naked.)

SEVERE SPANKING - This type of spanking can cause much redness and/or severe bruising (marking), blistering or worse on the buttocks of most spankees. The spankee likely will find sitting a challenge for a certain amount of time. This needs to be done in a consensual manner and might not be legal.

SILENT SPANKING – (1) When the spankee is not allowed to utter any noise while being spanked. (2) Alternatives to spanking that quietly give the butt pain, such as the application of capsicum cream (but a very small amount) and the less effective Tiger Balm. Do not put it on the anus or sex organs.

SLAVE SPANKING – See *Servant Spanking*. (1) In the modern world of BDSM (*Bondage, Domination, Sadism and Masochism*) the submissive person is called a slave and is under the influence and/or control of the dominate party typically called the "Master" (if male) or "Mistress" if female. The submissive slave is dominated and spanked when the dominant feels it is necessary for discipline and/or pleasure. (2) (See *Servant Spanking* for more on this part of the definition.) Slaves in ancient times often were considered part of the family. They may have been expressly gotten for purposes of physical and sexual pleasure. They were spanked publically and privately in Roman and Greek locations at the whim of their owners. In the more modern slave ownership period including the Caribbean and in North America, black slave girls would also be used for sexual gratification when their owners wanted it. Also other male slaves might spank other slaves for various reasons, particularly when they were a supervisor.

SLIPPERING - Using a slipper as the spanking implement.

SOOTHING CREAM – (Cold Cream) - A cream applied to a well spanked bottom to limit the sensation of pain.

SOUND SPANKING – See *Hard Spanking*.

SPANKABLE – (Spankworthy) – The person is well suited to be spanked. They may appear to have an ass, due to its shape and/or appearance, that appears particularly well designed to be spanked. The mannerisms of the person should scream "spank me"! A professional spanking actress should have great "spankability".

SPANKED TO TEARS – When the spankee is spanked hard enough to cry real tears. Bad girl!

SPANKFEST – A synonym for "Spank Feast". This is a gathering, public or private, where spanking is one of the primary events (or at least is publicized to be.)

SPANKING ART - (Spanking Comics) – Spanking themed art.

SPANKING AGREEMENT - An oral or written agreement regarding spanking related activities. See *Spanking Contracts*.

SPANKING BEGINNERS – *Spanking Beginners* typically have little or no significant experience with giving a spanking and/or receiving a spanking.

It's important that the beginner's first spanking (or first few spankings) are as positive an experience as possible. Does the spankee want it to be a sexual experience also, if so then make sure sexual stimulation is accented. A bad experience now could turn this person off from spanking and another butt is lost to the spanking world :(

SPANKING BLOG – A (preferably) regularly updated online diary/web magazine that individuals and organizations keep regarding spanking pursuits.

SPANKING BONDAGE - When bondage is included with the spanking. Typically this means that the spankee is securely tied down and immobile for his/her spanking. Perhaps he/she is tied down to a piece of spanking furniture.

SPANKING CLUB – These associations provide a way to meet and/or otherwise intertwine with others in the spanking scene. They're sometimes called "Munches". Spanking clubs have grown quite a bit in number in recent years.

SPANKING CONTEST – When couples compete with spankings for a prize or prizes. The rules vary from contest to contest. Possibly included are:

A) Extra points for the spankee with the reddest butt
B) Extra points for the nicest looking marks
C) Points deducted for blistering or appearance of blood (typically then the spanking is over for them anyway)
D) Extra points for sexiest spankee's behavior while being spanked.
E) Points deducted for the spankee trying to block blows or get away
F) Points deducted for the spanker tiring too quickly
G) Extra points for the spankee with the sexist outfit and/or the outfit most conducive to making the spanking easier
H) Extra points for the spanker/spankee couple that is the most fun to listen to during the spanking
I) Extra points for how sexy and submissive the spankee is during and at the end of the spanking. She will have to beg for forgiveness, etc.
J) Extra points to the couple that uses the most spanking implements during the spanking
K) Extra points to the spankee's bottom that feels the best after being well spanked.
L) Extra points to the spankee that gets the most aroused
M) Extra points for the spankee with the most spanks during that time period.

Multiple spankings can be going on at the same time. Also see *Duel Spanking*.

SPANKING CONTRACT - It's a good idea for the participants to sit down and talk about their spanking scenarios, including under what circumstances the spanking will take place, how the spanking will be delivered, number of swats, instruments to be used, position of the person to be spanked, whether spanked with clothing on or bare bottom, etc. All participants then have an oral agreement on the terms, or have a signed written contract on the terms. This author sells a *Spanking Contract* through your ebookstore.

SPANKING CURRENCY - This is when spanks take the place of money, more specifically in place of your country's currency. How many spanks do you have in your spanking account? What are you going to buy with them? Or perhaps you are making a trade? Do you have a debt to pay off?

A common "spanking currency" scenario is paying off a debt. The spankee gets spanked in exchange for the debt.

SPANKING DANCE –The sub/slave does a sexy dance in front of her dominant and is spanked at various parts (times) of her dance. Perhaps it's after the end of each song, or if her dancing is not of an acceptable nature.

SPANKING DEMONSTRATION - When spanking partners demonstrate various aspects of spanking, including spanking implements and the best ways to spank.

SPANKING ENTHUSIAST – (Spankophile) - Someone who enjoys spanking, either receiving or giving. This includes activities related to spanking such as spanking media, building spanking furniture and spanking modeling.

SPANKING FANTASY – (Spanking Fantasies) – Mental images that run through one's head associated with spanking. A great many people have these.

SPANKING FOR COUPLES – Adult spanking activities that couples involve themselves in.

SPANKING FURNITURE – These apparatuses are used to place and secure one or more spankees. These include whipping benches, the spanking horse, the birching horse and the spanking bench. The spankee may or may not be tied down to it. The spankee often will find him or herself in the kneeling position or bent-over position. There should be easy access to their buttocks and often spanking furniture make the buttocks the most elevated portion of the spankee's body. Also being able to take and/or play with the spankee sexually while on and/or tied to spanking furniture is of pronounced importance.

SPANKING GAMES – (1) Online interactive games where the players determine who gets spanked and the intensity of the spankings. A spanking game may let the player interactively spank one or more characters. (2) Physical games such as Strip Poker that calls for one or more participants being spanked at various intervals. This type of spanking game typically has a way of determining who the spankee is and who the spanker is.

SPANKING HOST – The host or hostess at spanking social events and online and real-life spanking clubs.

SPANKING IMPLEMENTS – These physical devices are used to aid and enhance the delivery of the spanking blows. Examples include paddles, straps, slappers, floggers, rods, switches, canes, spanksticks, crops, the tawse and whips. Not everybody agrees but some people feel this category also includes restraint aids such as handcuffs and rope.

SPANKING LIFESTYLE – The world of spanking is innately intertwined into the lives of the spanker and/or spankee.

SPANKING MAGAZINE – Content from these wonderful periodicals now are often also online.

SPANKING MASSAGES – Combining full or partial body massages with spankings. The massaging may be the primary activity or vice versa.

SPANKING MASTURBATION – (1) Masturbating during and/or after a spanking and masturbating on those days afterwards while your bottom is still sore from the spanking. (2) Being spanked for masturbating.

SPANKING ORGASM – An orgasm that is obtained while one is being spanked, or while their buttock is still smarting from having been spanked in hours or days since the spanking.

SPANKING PARTY – Spanking parties might be in a home, a hotels or resort and are a gatherings specifically set up to accommodate spanking. Often there tends to be a significantly higher percentage of males at these events than females.

SPANKING POSITIONS – The bodily location of spanker and spankee just prior to, during and just after the spanking.

SPANKING PRACTIONER – See *Spanking Enthusiast*.

SPANKING REMINDER – This often is a short but relatively intense spanking session to make sure the spankee remembers to be obedient and/or is reminded as to what kind of punishment awaits her should she do something wrong.

SPANKING ROLEPLAY - There are many role-play scenarios that can include spanking. Naughty nurse, submissive maid, naughty schoolgirl, misbehaving cheerleader and warden/prisoner role playing is popular with male dominants and female submissives.

Spanking Roleplaying can require acting and props but it always includes a generous helpings of spankings.

SPANKING SERIES – A sequence and/or collection of spankings and/or spanking characters, stories, videos and/or pictures, which have certain characteristics in common.

SPANKING SESSION – Most associated with visits to FemDoms and Spanking Therapists. These are often "visits" that have a purpose but it still can be just a girlfriend and boyfriend meeting for fun.

SPANKING STICK – These look a lot like manmade canes.

SPANKING STORIES – (*Spanking Novels, Spanking Novellas, Spanking Series, Corporal Punishment Fiction, Flagellation Erotica, Romantic Spanking Stories*) – These are literature adventures involving spanking. These go back to the 1700s and may or may not involve sexual activities. The Marquis de Sade is among the most famous of these authors. In the past these tended to be clandestine publications that were sold secretly.

SPANKING THERAPIST – A person that administers *Spanking Therapy*.

SPANKING THERAPY – This aims to help spankees improve themselves. Perhaps he/she needs more motivation or just the tension release of a good spanking. The spanking is conducted by a professional. The spankee's needs are assessed and addressed in a controlled, nurturing environment (assuming nurturing is what the spankee wants.)

SPANKING VIDEOS – Spanking videos have proliferated with the Internet. As is obvious, these videos show spankees getting spanked and often dominated in other ways.

SPANKING WITH ANAL STIMULATION – (1) Directly stimulating the anus while giving a spanking (which can include aiming the blows at the anus and/or to make the blows include the anus.) It can occur before a spanking, and/or in between spankings, and/or after a spanking. This might involve inserting a butt plug (inflatable or otherwise), finger(s), anal vibrator, a dildo, or rectal thermometer into the anus. It might include carefully spanking a dildo that's already put into the anus to make it move up and down in the anus as blows are applied to it and the buttocks. (2) Actually spanking the anus with a narrow spanking instrument. (Spanking related enemas are a separate subject, see *Enema Spanking*.

Anal stimulation doesn't necessarily include anal intercourse.

SPANKING THE MONKEY – Male masturbation.

SPANKOPHILE – – (*aka Spanking Enthusiast*) - Someone who enjoys spanking, either receiving or giving. Their interest could also include spanking implements, discussing spanking, spanking media, building spanking furniture and spanking modeling.

SPENCER SPANKING PLAN – A well known domestic discipline spanking contract that originated in the 1930s.

STING AND THUD - Thinner spanking instruments such as switches release their energy closer to the skin and thus 'sting' more. Thicker spanking instruments such as paddles release their energy down further in the buttocks making more of a "thud" sensation.

STRAP – (aka *Leather Strap*) – A spanking instrument of various sizes that can be deliciously effective. It's often made of leather and thus is pliable.

STRESS RELIEF SPANKING – (*Tension Relief Spanking*) - The aim of these spankings are to eliminate frustration and guilt and cleanse oneself mentally. At the conclusion of these spankings relaxation and comfort can be had by the spankee.

STRUGGLING – When the spankee fails to hold his/herself adequately in place for/during and after their spanking.

SUBMISSIVE SPANKING – When the spankee wants to feel dominated as part of the spanking, over and above the domination involved with him/her getting spanked.

SUBMIT AND OBEY – A Dom/sub lifestyle outlook where the submissive submits and obeys his/her Dominant.

SWITCH SPANKING – Where the spanker and spankee take turns spanking each other.

SWITCHING – (Associated with Birching) – A switch is a flexible thin branch (rod) from one or more trees. (A collection of thin branches can be tied together to also be used as a spanking implement.) A switch is applied with force to the buttocks of the spankee. The switch like the cane can hurt more than many other spanking implements due to its thinner surface area so caution is advised. Also see *Caning*.

TENDER – The tendency for the buttocks to become sensitive to the touch after a good spanking.

TENSION RELIEF SPANKING – See *Stress Relief Spanking*.

THRASHING – This term is more popular in England and denotes a hard spanking/beating often with one or more implements.

TICKLE SPANKING – (1) Tickling the buttocks and then spanking it (an act that can be repeated.) (2) Tickling various parts of a person's body such as their belly and the bottoms of their feet, and also spanking that person's buttocks, alternatively or simultaneously.

TIT WHIPPING – Spanking the breasts of a woman using one or more implements. This can only be done consensually and with caution.

TRADITIONAL SPANKING – This denotes standard methods of spanking. No unusual methods of buttocal pain infliction, such as *Silent Spanking*, would be included in this category.

TOP UP SPANKING – These are given regularly, even every few days, even in addition to any other spankings the spankee has received. These spankings are for bad behavior that the spankee got away with during that time period (say week) and for bad behavior she might be tempted to do in the following week. See *Maintenance Spanking*.

TOUCH-YOUR-TOES – When in a standing position the spankee may be ordered to reach down and touch as close to their toes (perhaps their knees) as possible so their buttocks can tighten and stick out thus becoming an easier target to spank.

TOUGHEN-UP SPANKING – These spankings (and spankings in general) if given with regularity, can dull nerve endings in the buttocks as well as toughen tissues in the buttocks. The spankee might evolve into having a "leather butt" which is a butt that can take a disproportionately hard spanking.

WAKE-UP SPANKING – This well helps to wake up sleepy beauty and typically works much better than an alarm clock.

WARM-UP SPANKING - This is a light spanking, often by hand and perhaps on a clothed bottom, before the "real" and more intense spanking begins. Its purpose is to prepare the butt for the coming onslaught.

WEARS HER (HIS) MARKS WITH PRIDE – (*Spanking Marks*) – A good spanking with more than moderate intensity (depending on how sensitive the spankee's bottom is) can leave the bottom a lovely shade of red. It also can leave light contusions and more significant bruises. These bruises (aka "marks") could remain for days or longer or they can be gone in hours. A spankophile is proud of these marks hence the phrase "wears her (his) marks with pride".

WEIGHT-LOSS SPANKING – If the spankee needs motivation to lose weight, spanking can be of use. The spankee can be spanked whenever weight loss goals are not reached and/or can have the more desirable reward of a pleasurable spanking when the goals are met. Perhaps the spankee should be given a hard spanking just before the diet is to begin to remind him/her what's in store if transgressions occur.

WELL-SPANKED BUTT – A buttocks that has the tell-tale signs of having gotten a good spanking.

WET SPANKING – For this the spankee's butt is made wet. It can also be when the spankee wears something wet that covers her bottom and is spanked over that. This can enhance the pain coefficient.

WHEEL BARROW SPANKING POSITION – The spanker sits up and the spankee lays her hands on the floor directly in front of the spanker. The spankee spreads her legs and brings her ass and legs up over the sitting spanker's lap. Her legs are positioned on each side of his upper torso. Her pussy and anus are spread wide open next to his midsection. Her ass cheeks are on his lap, her spread open pussy lips are facing him.

WHEEL BARROW SPANKING – When the entire spanking is administered with the spankee in the wheel barrow spanking position (see previous definition.)

WHUPPIN – Slang for whipping.

WOODEN SPOON – This kitchen implement can also double as a spanking implement. Bad girl!

The End